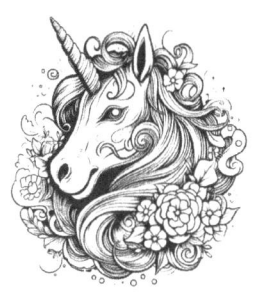
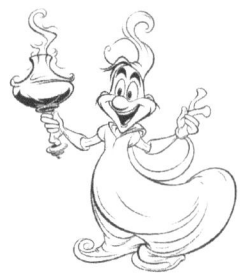

I0497896
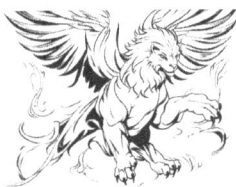
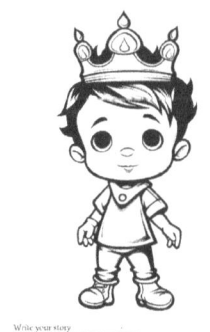
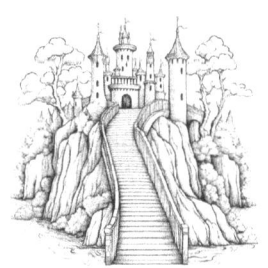
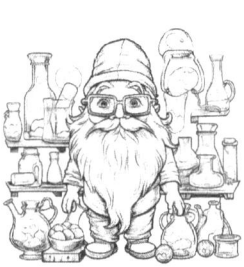
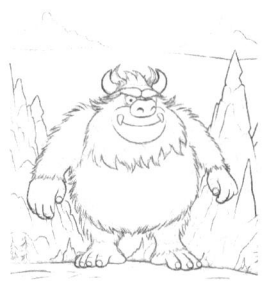
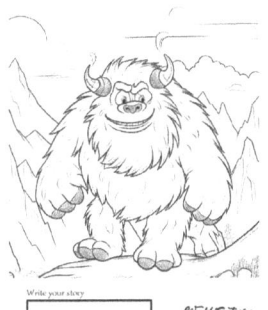
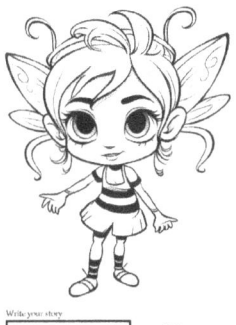
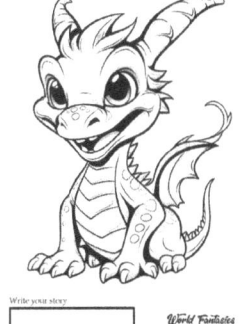

World Fantasies Coloring Book

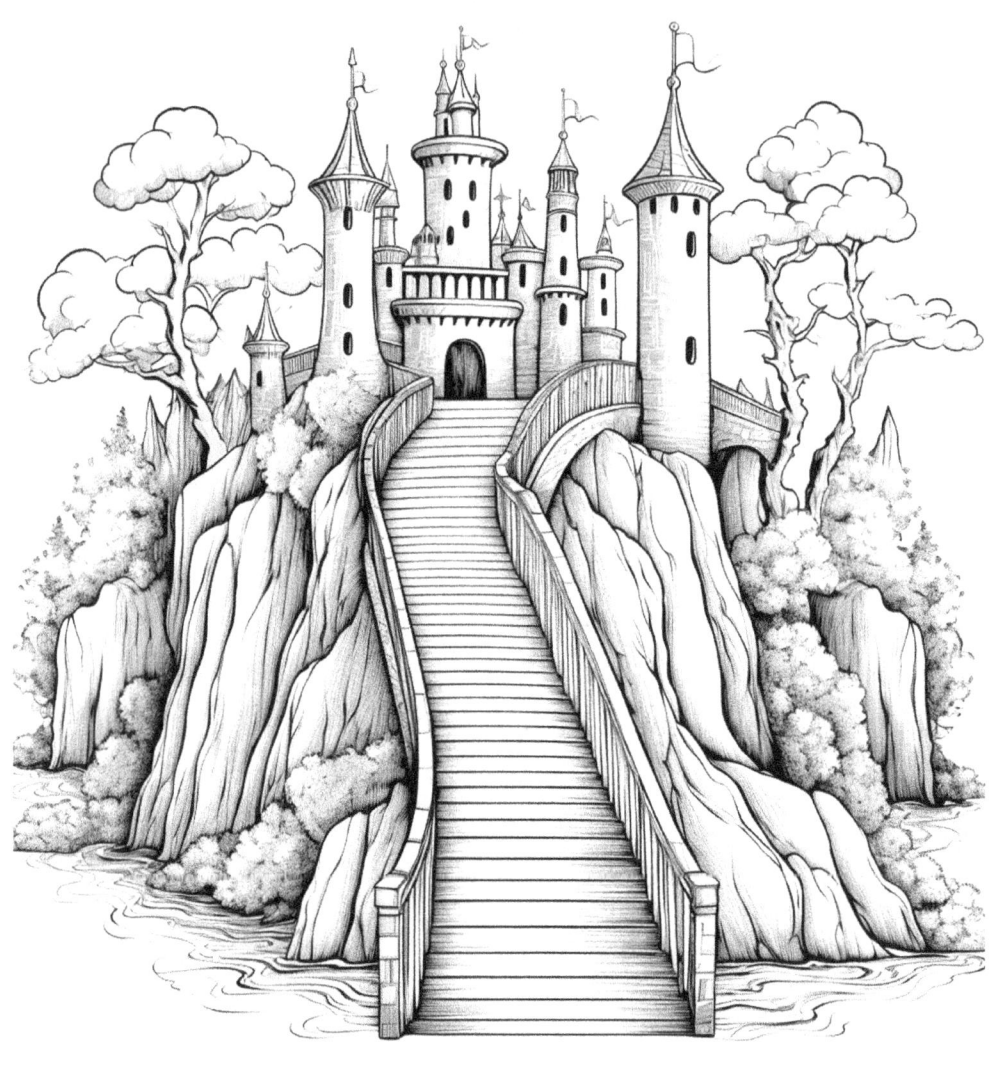

Write your story

World Fantasies Coloring Book

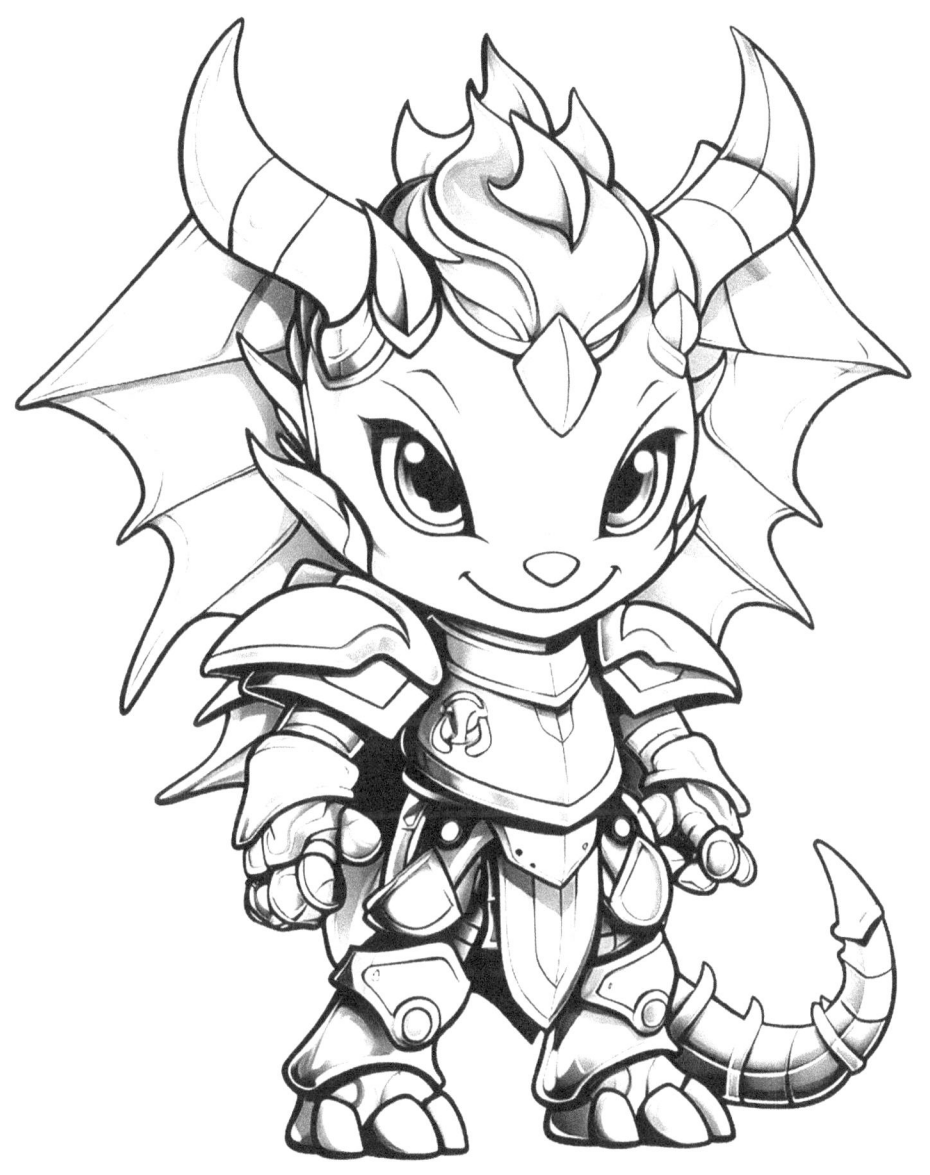

Write your story

World Fantasies
Coloring Book

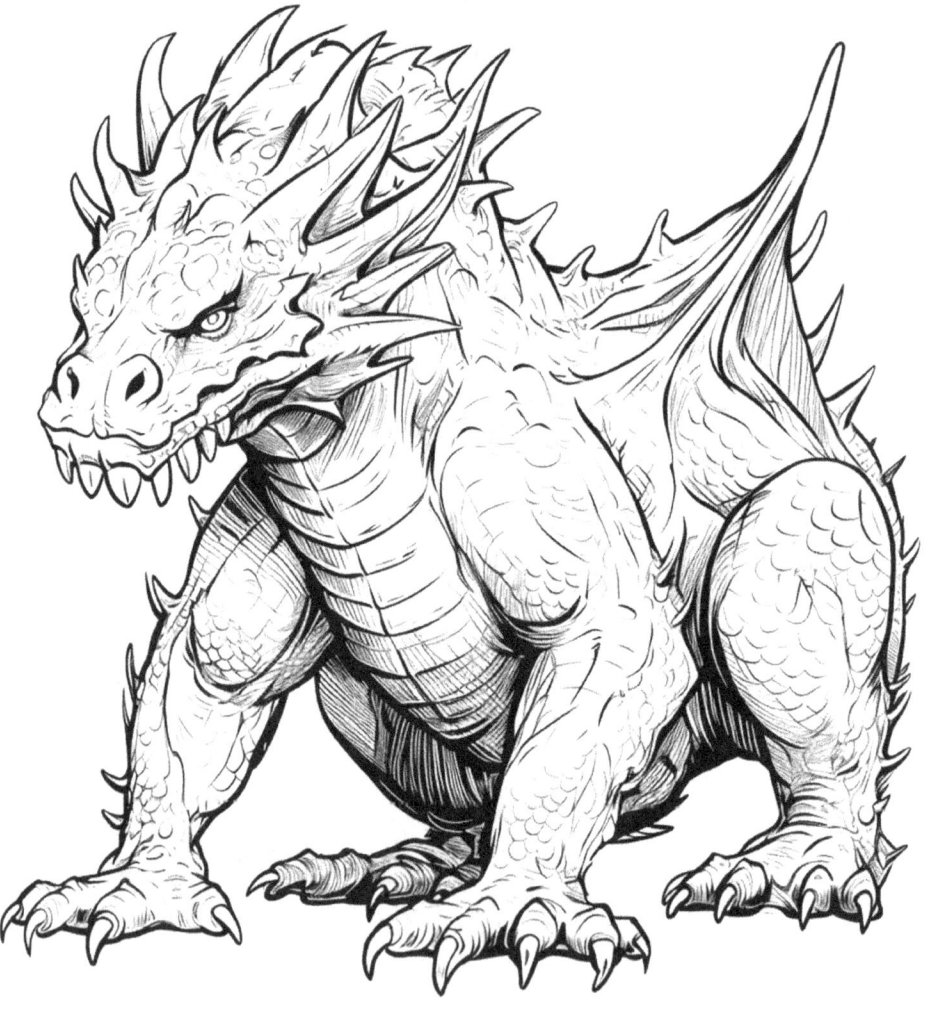

Write your story

World Fantasies Coloring Book

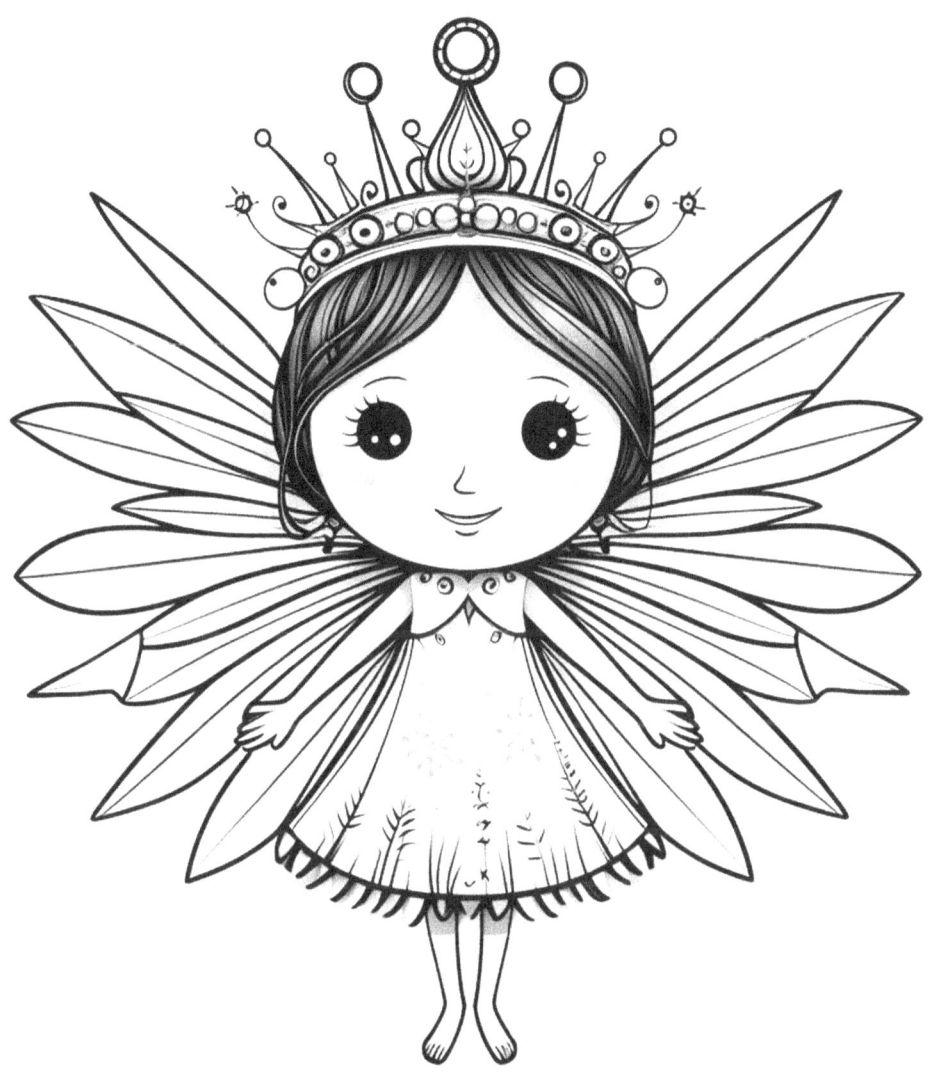

Write your story

World Fantasies Coloring Book

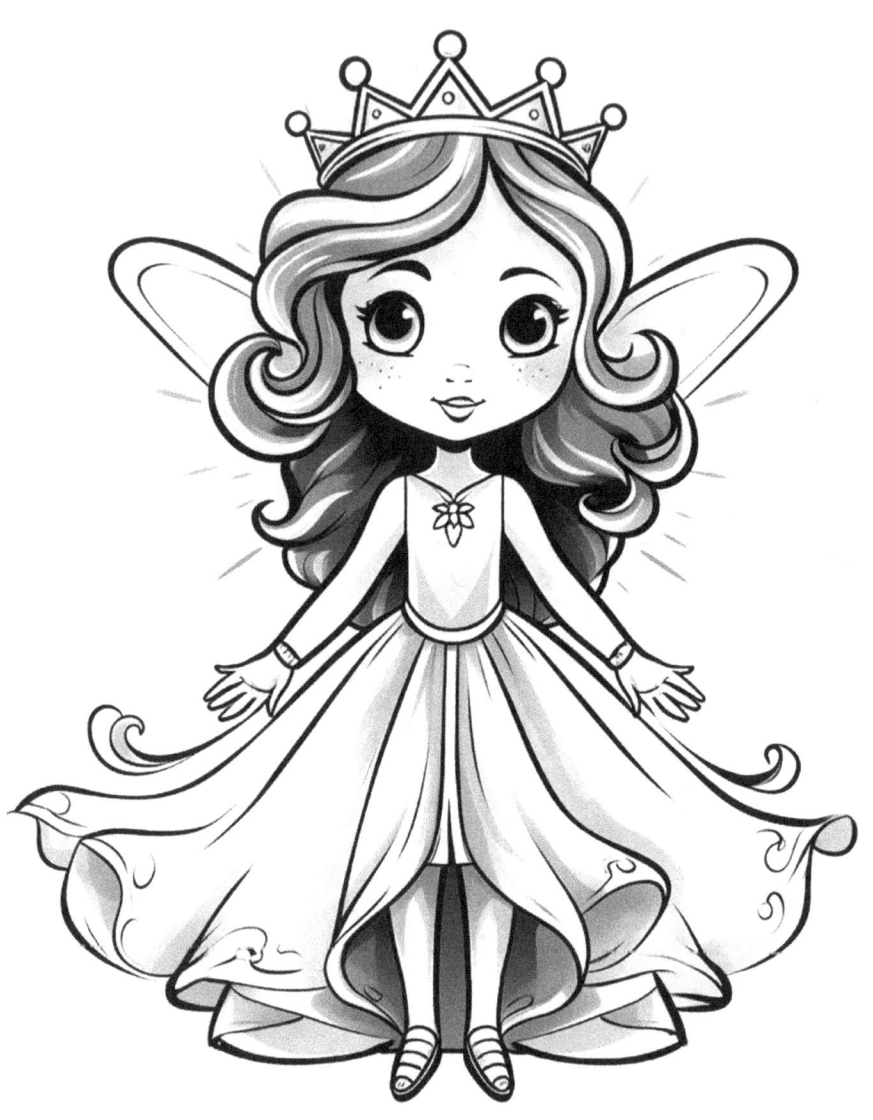

Write your story

World Fantasies
Coloring Book

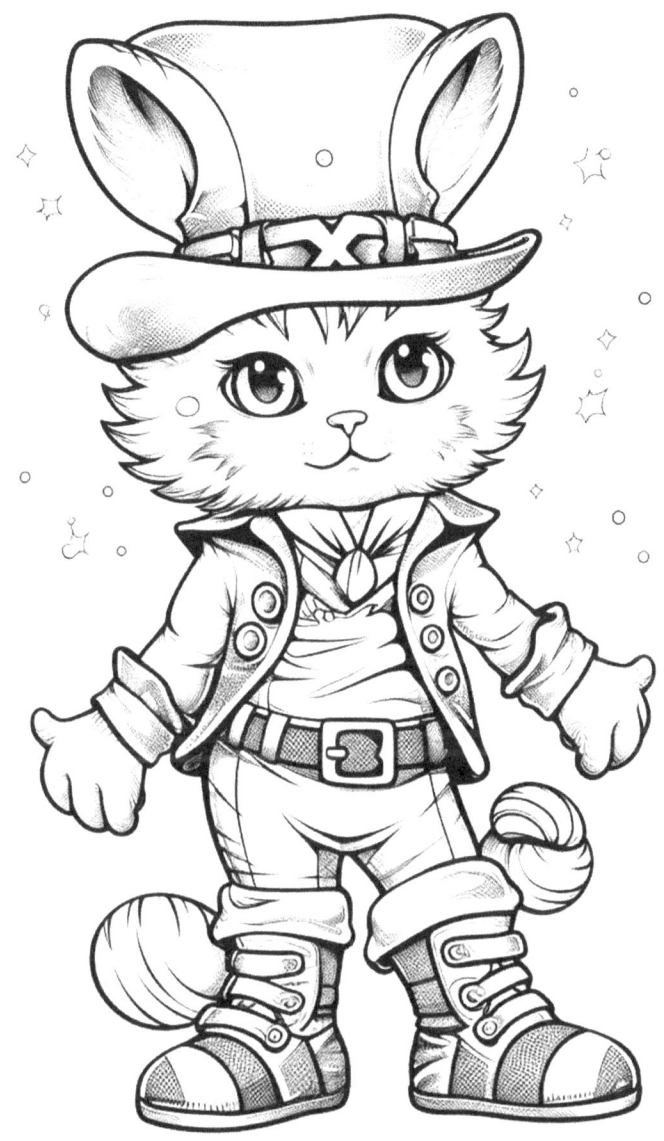

Write your story

World Fantasies Coloring Book

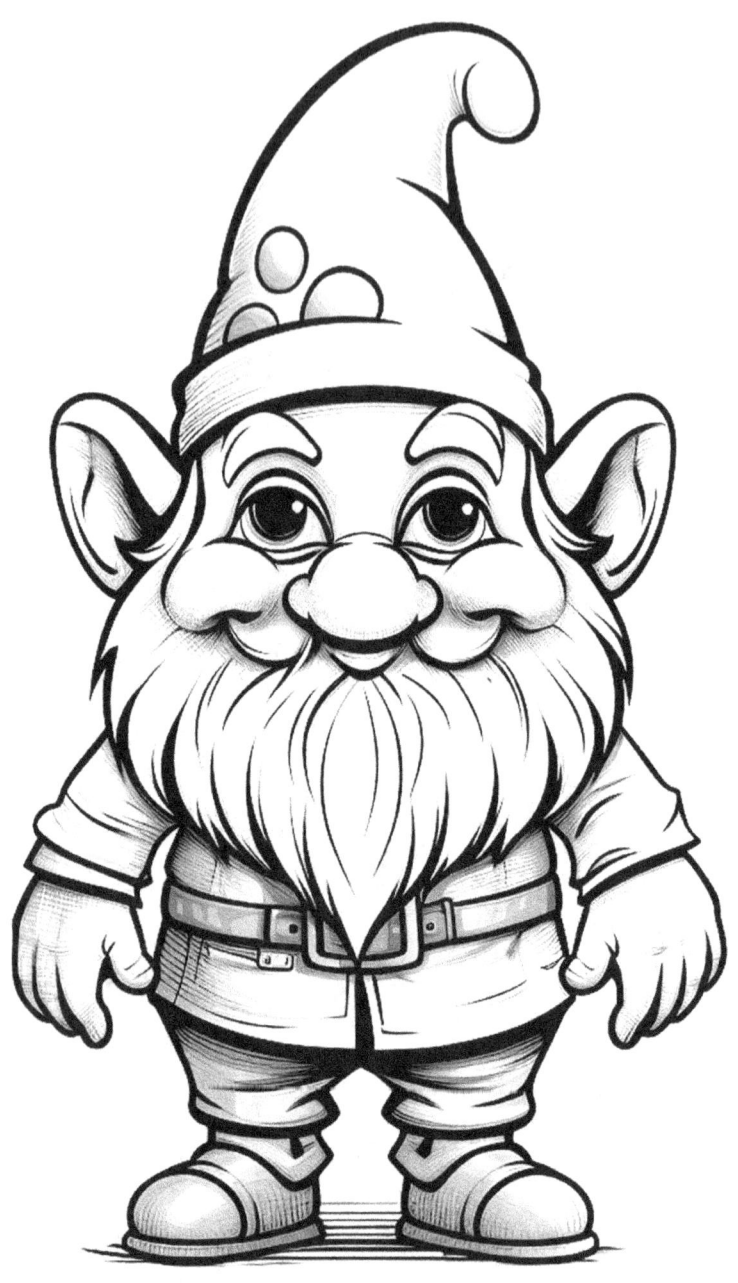

Write your story

World Fantasies Coloring Book

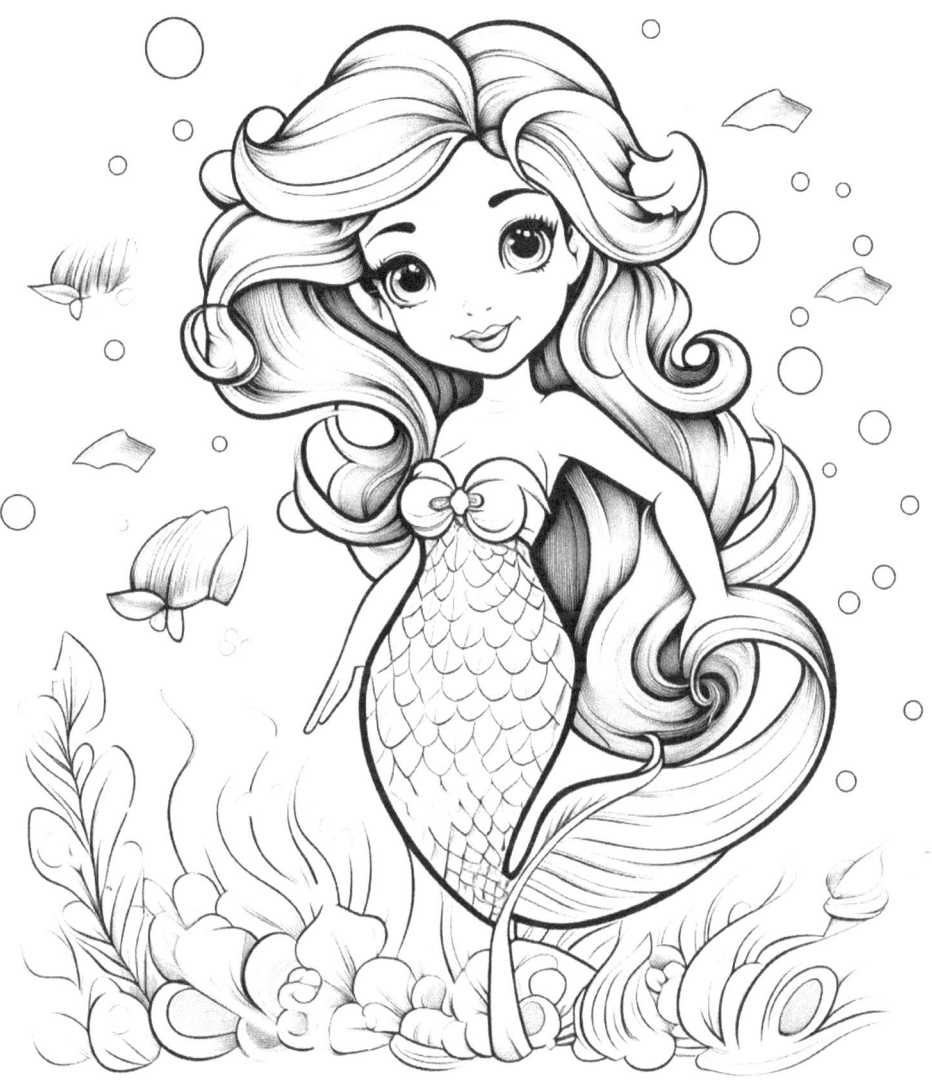

Write your story

World Fantasies Coloring Book

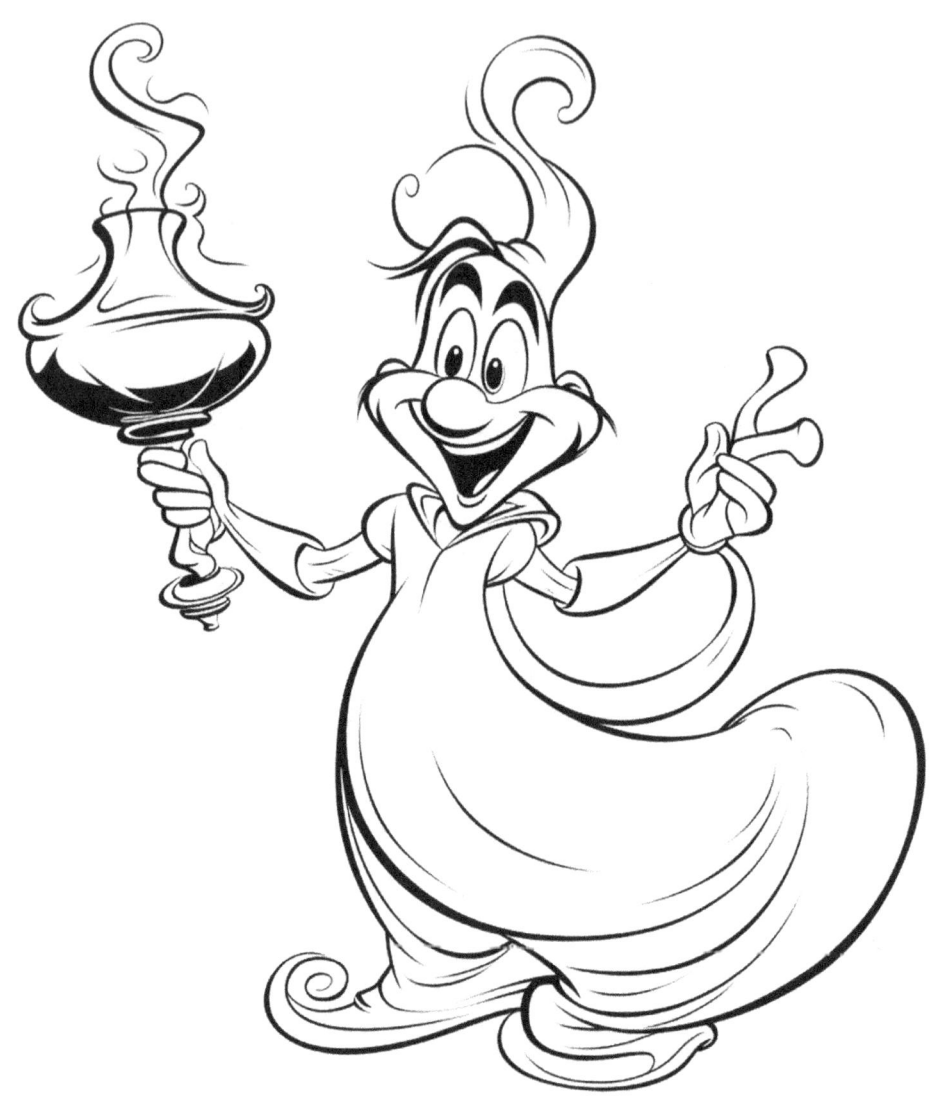

Write your story

World Fantasies Coloring Book

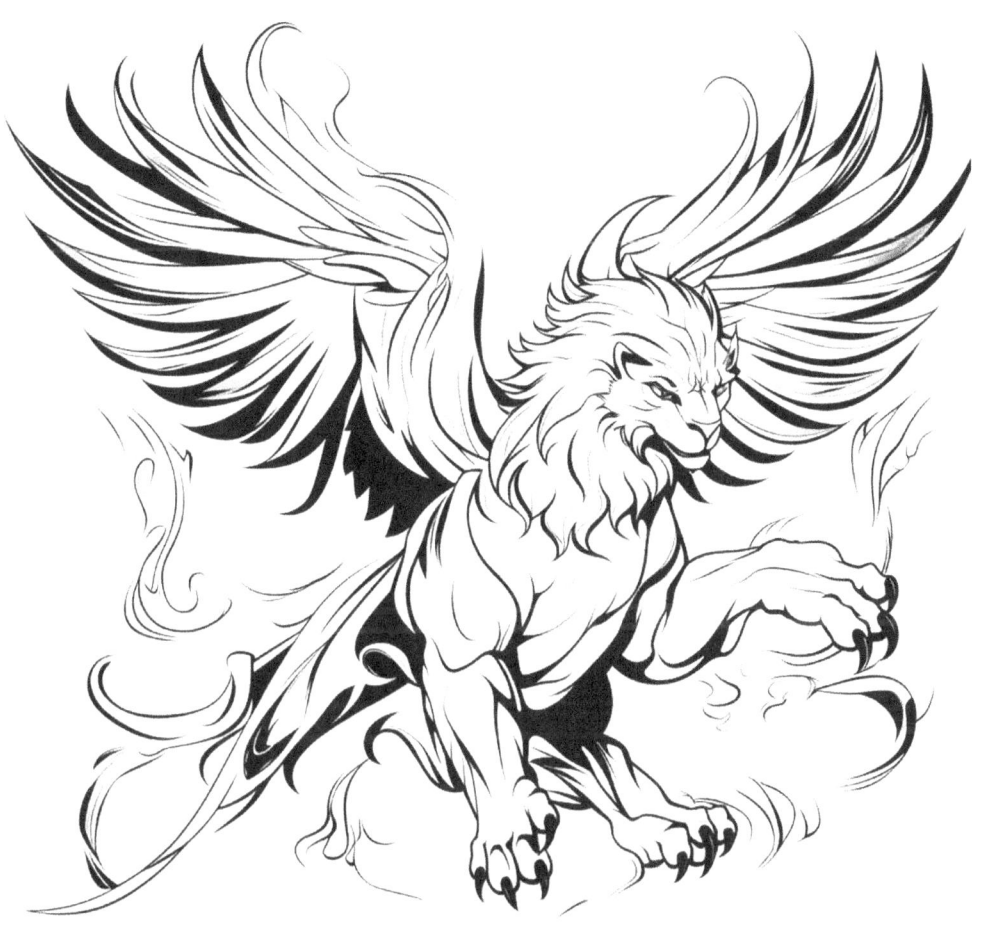

Write your story

World Fantasies Coloring Book

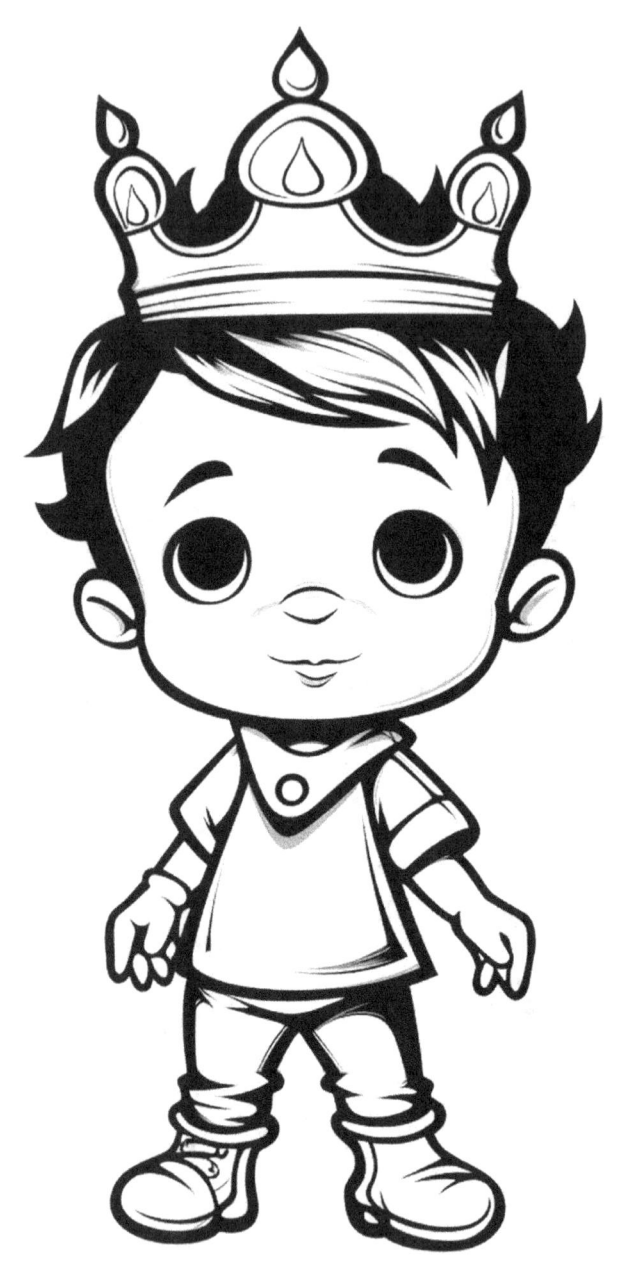

Write your story

World Fantasies Coloring Book

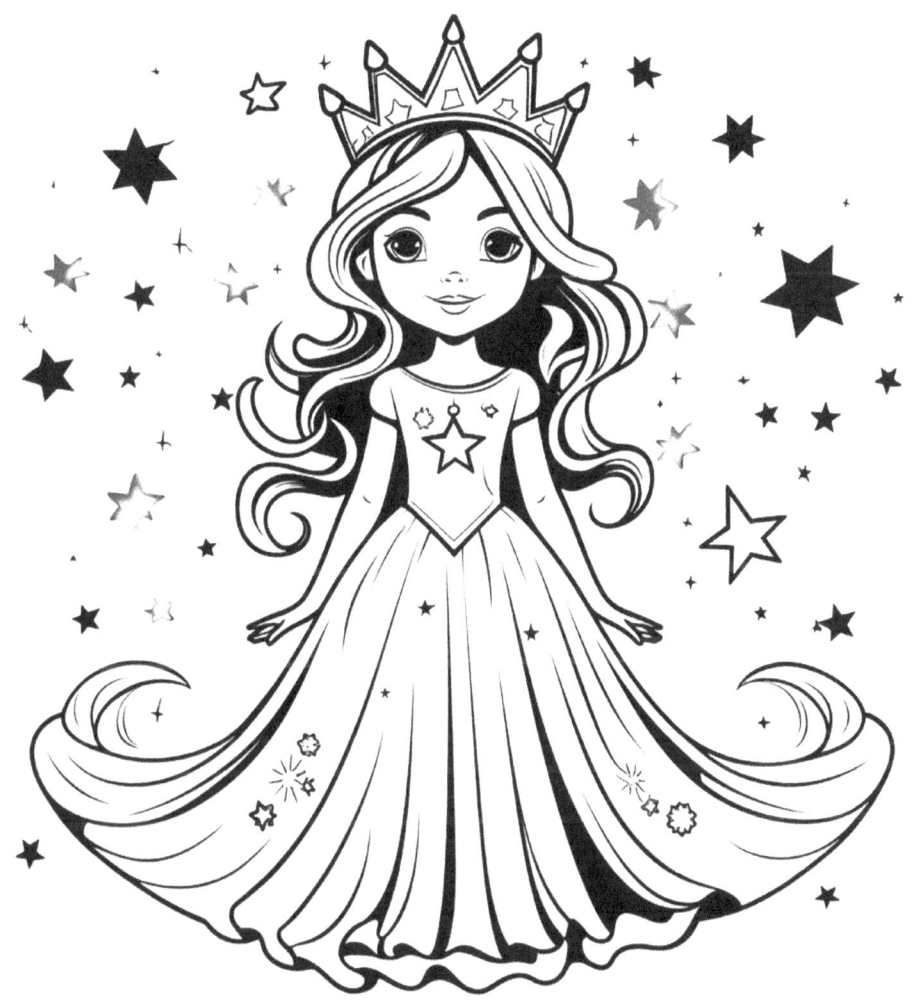

Write your story

World Fantasies Coloring Book

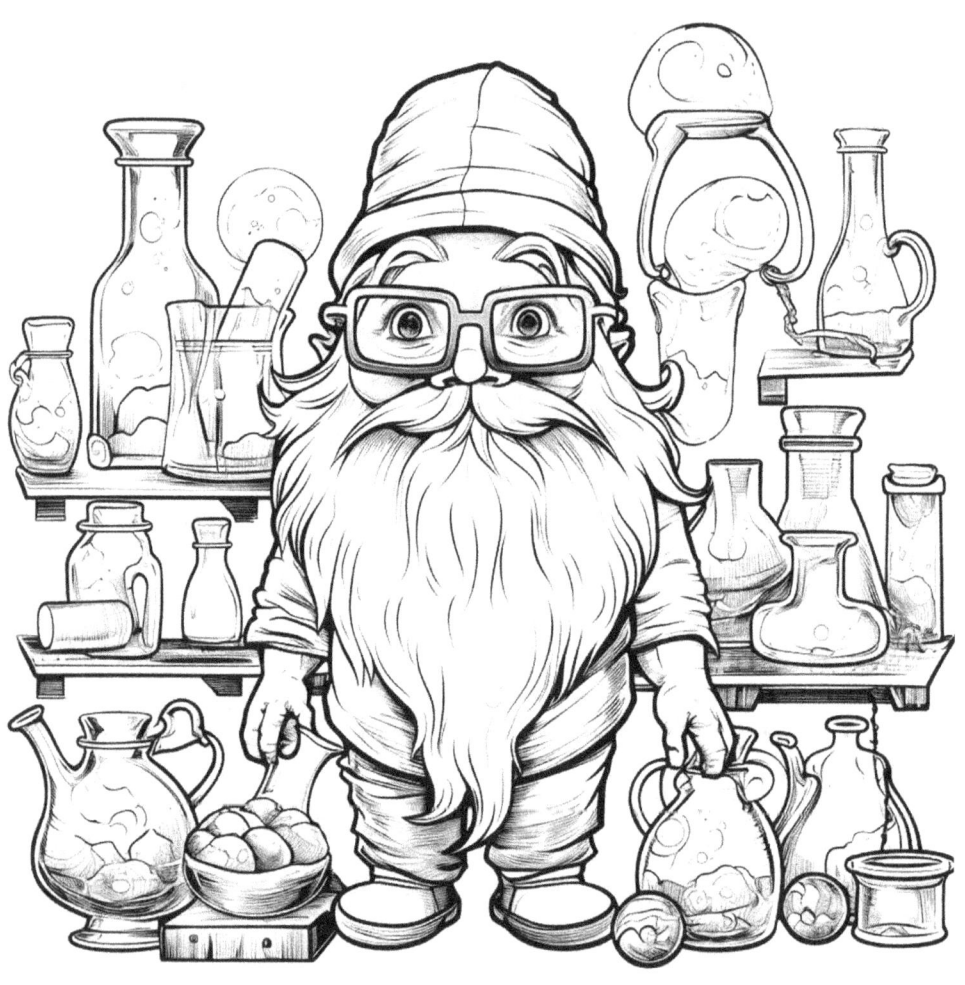

Write your story

World Fantasies Coloring Book

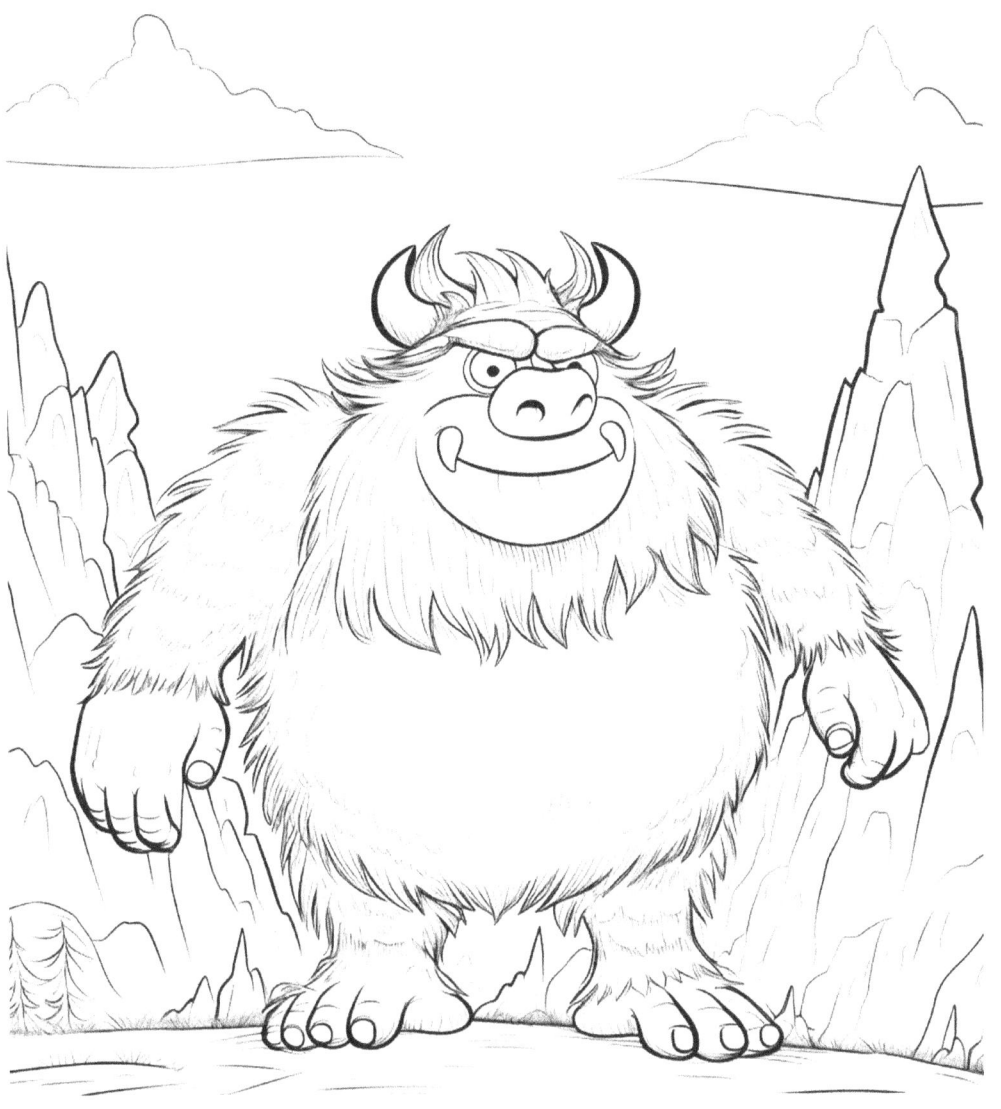

Write your story

World Fantasies Coloring Book

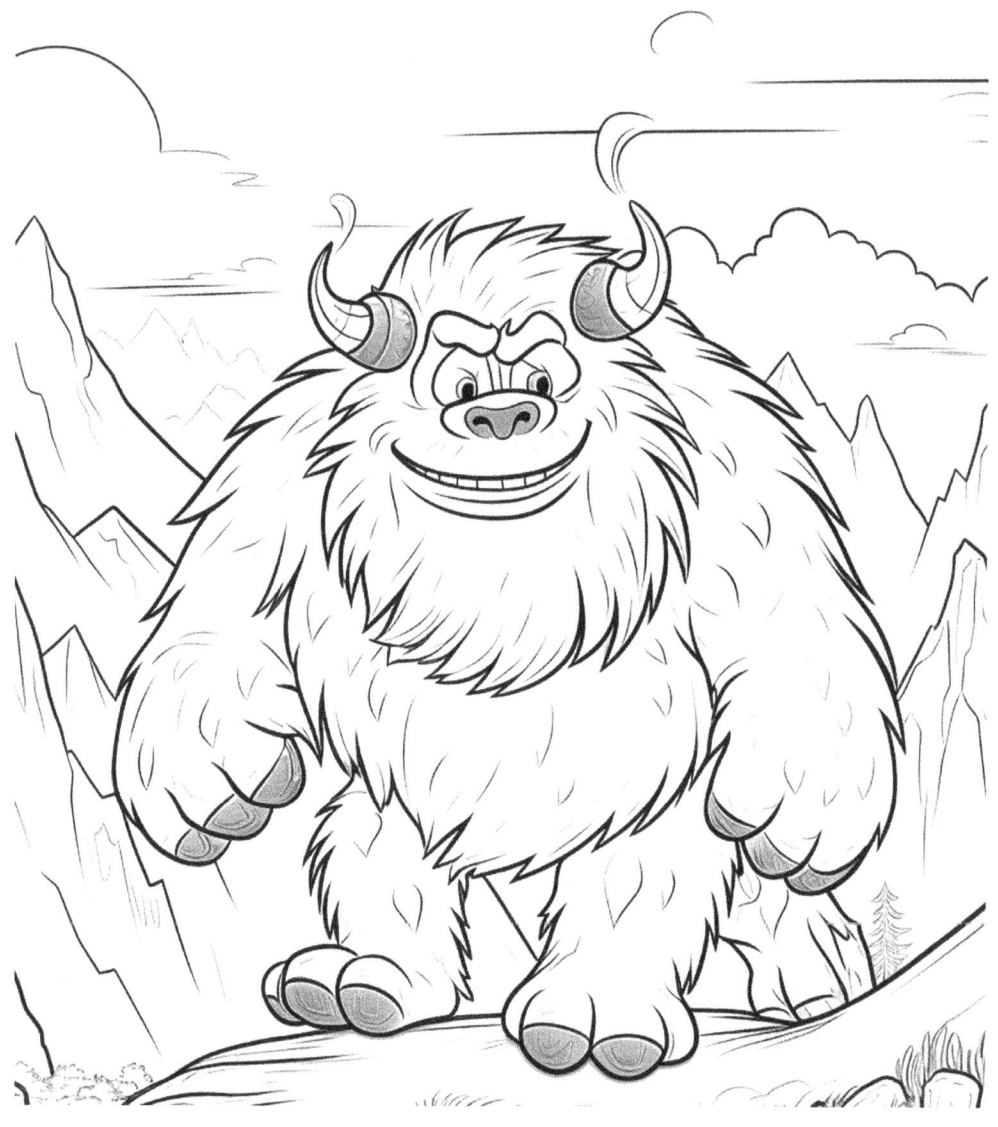

Write your story

World Fantasies Coloring Book

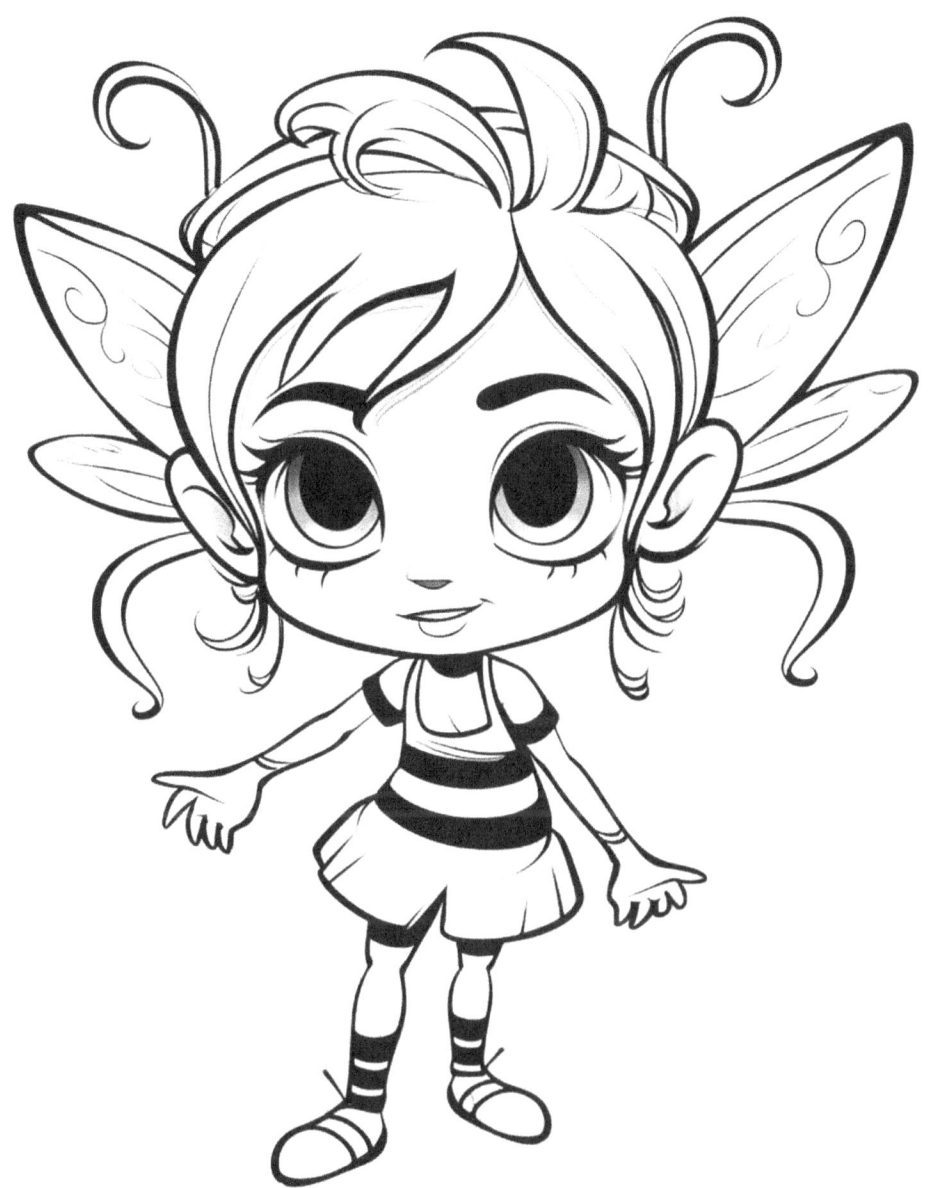

Write your story

World Fantasies
Coloring Book

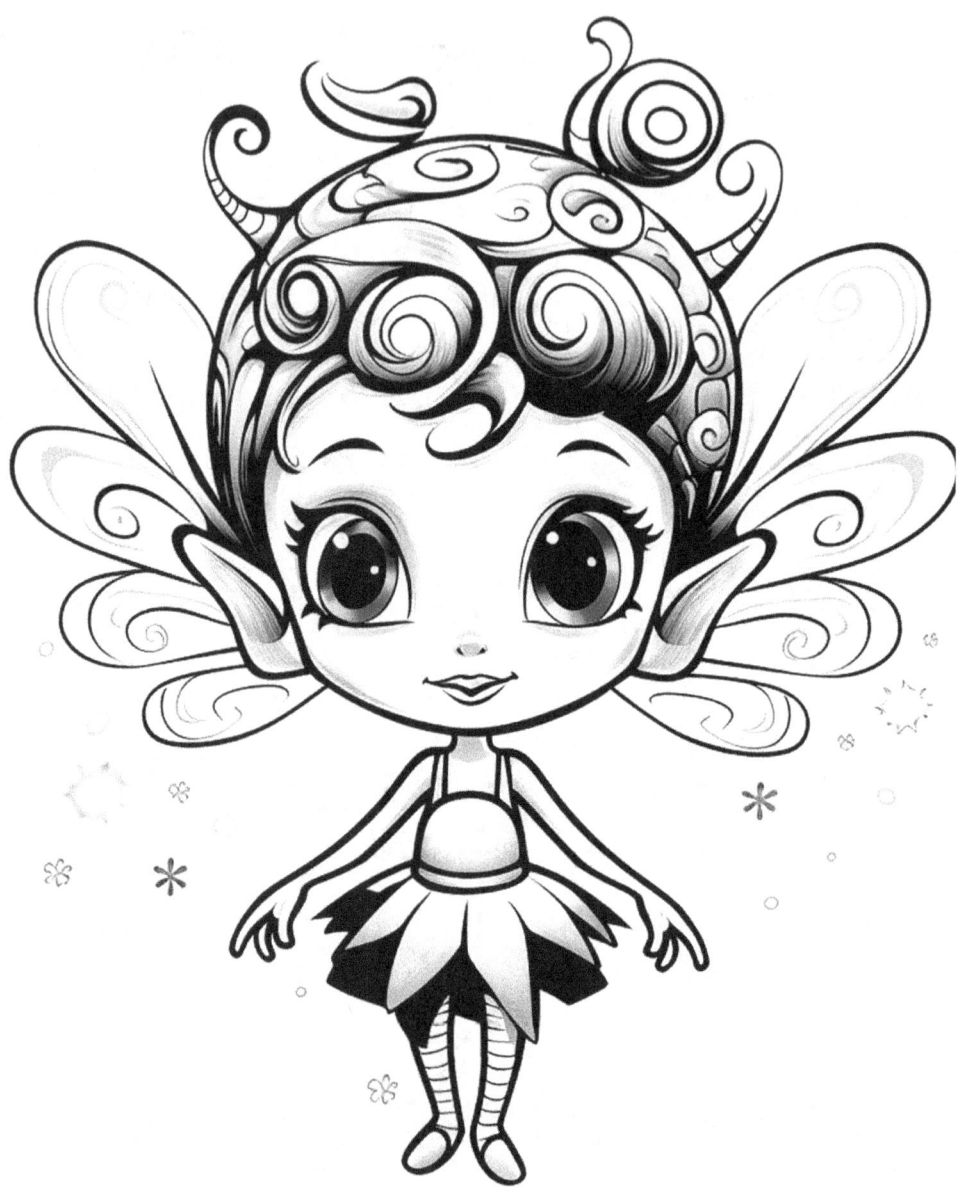

Write your story

World Fantasies Coloring Book

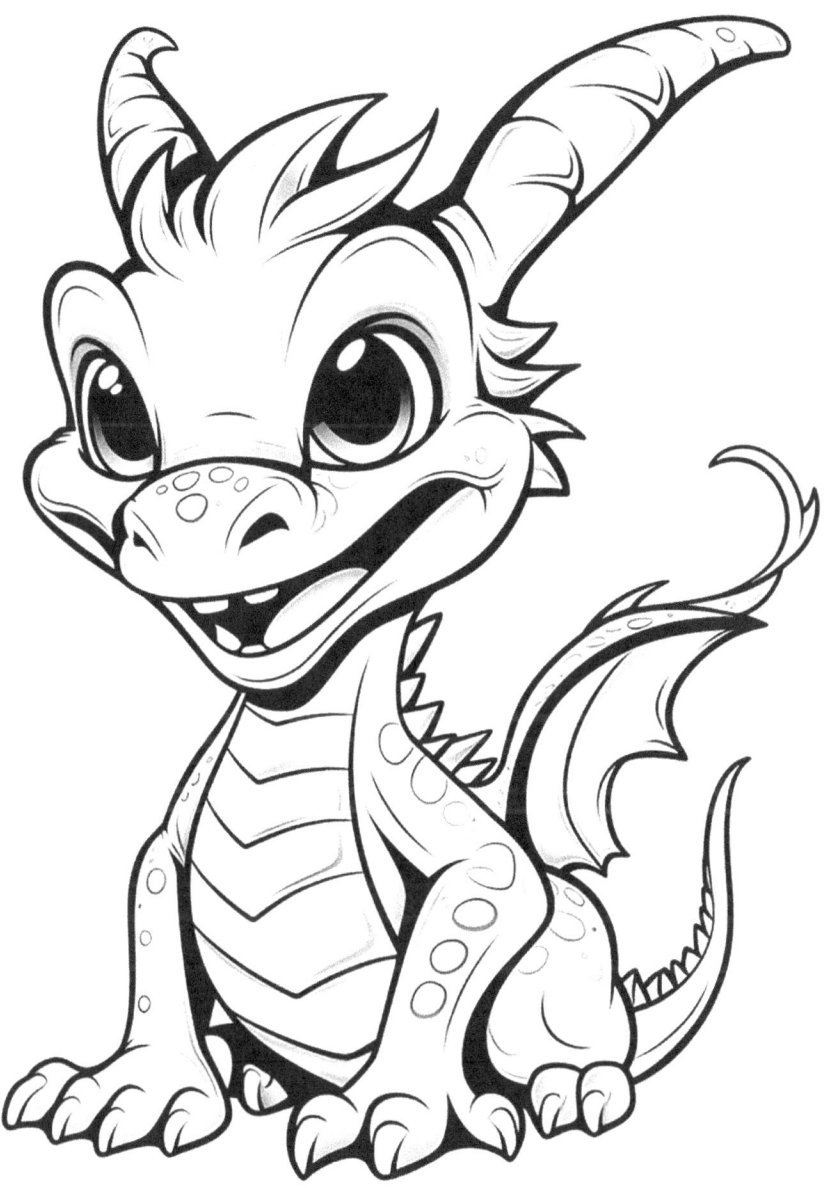

Write your story

World Fantasies
Coloring Book

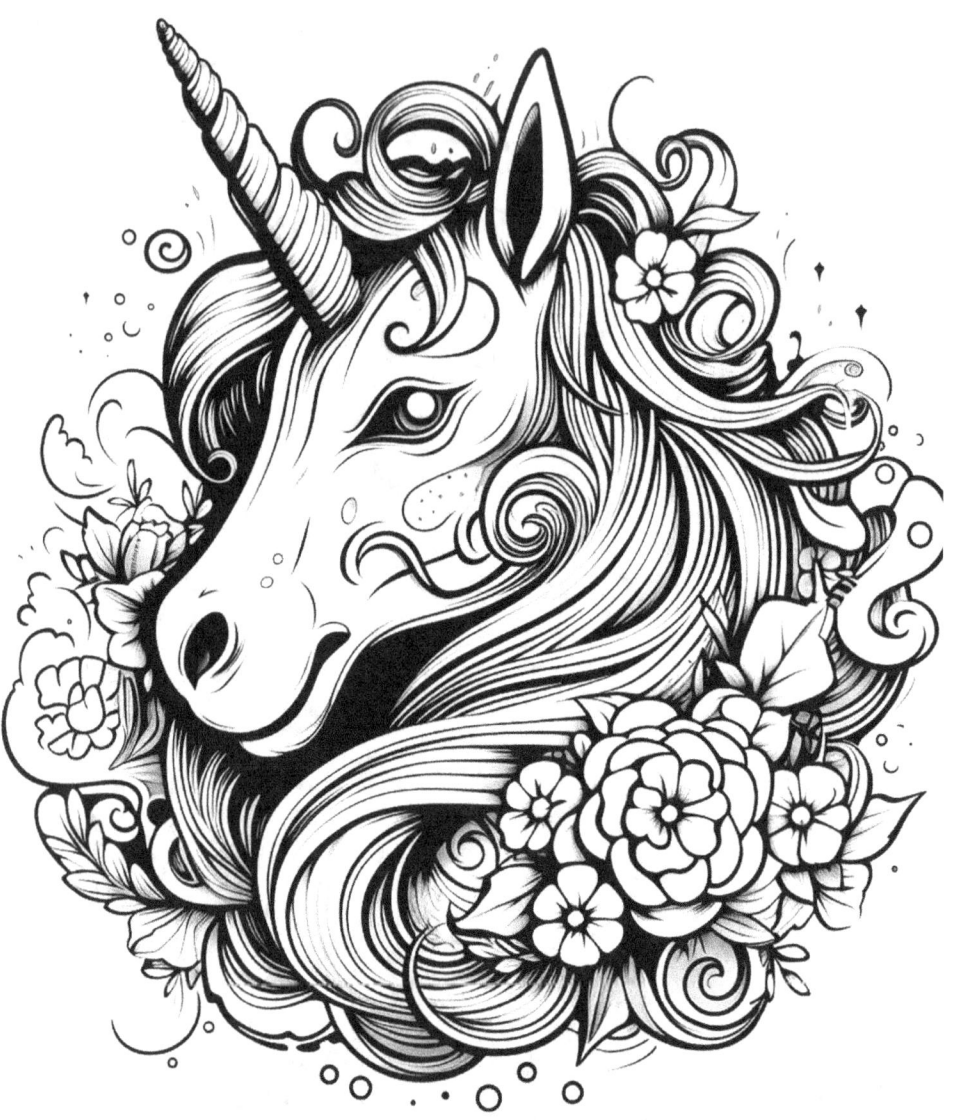

Write your story

World Fantasies Coloring Book

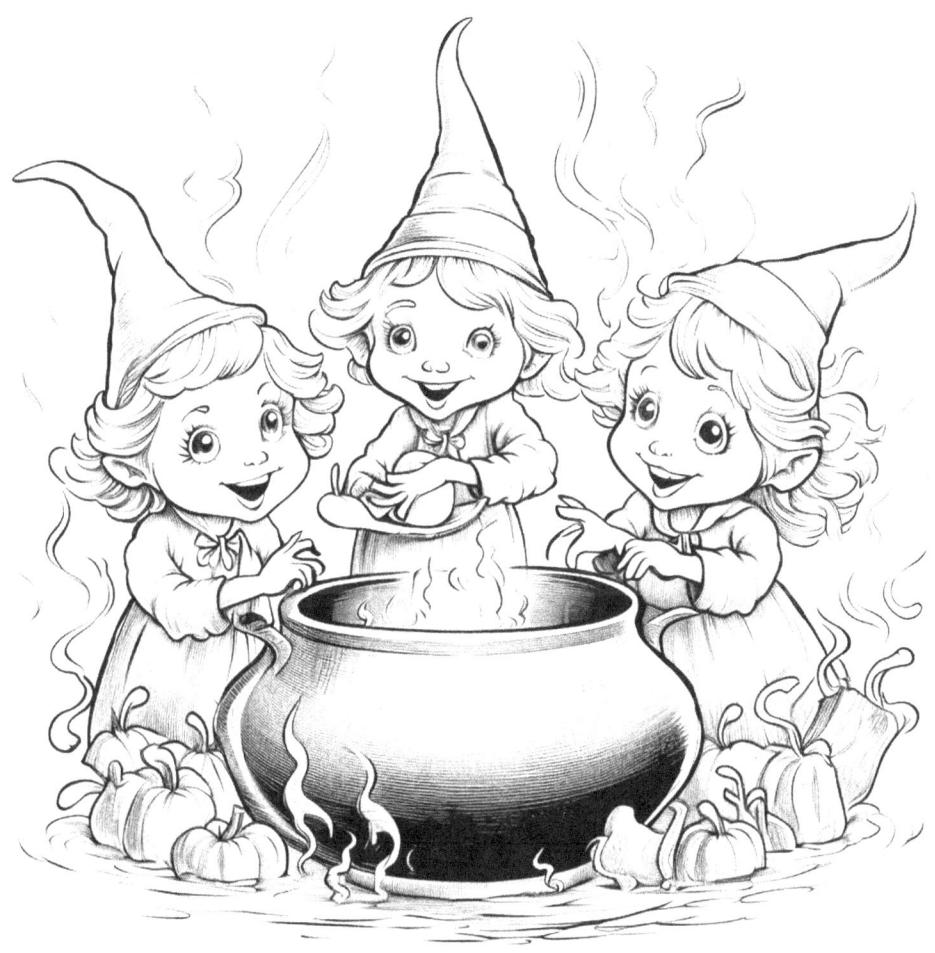

Write your story

World Fantasies Coloring Book

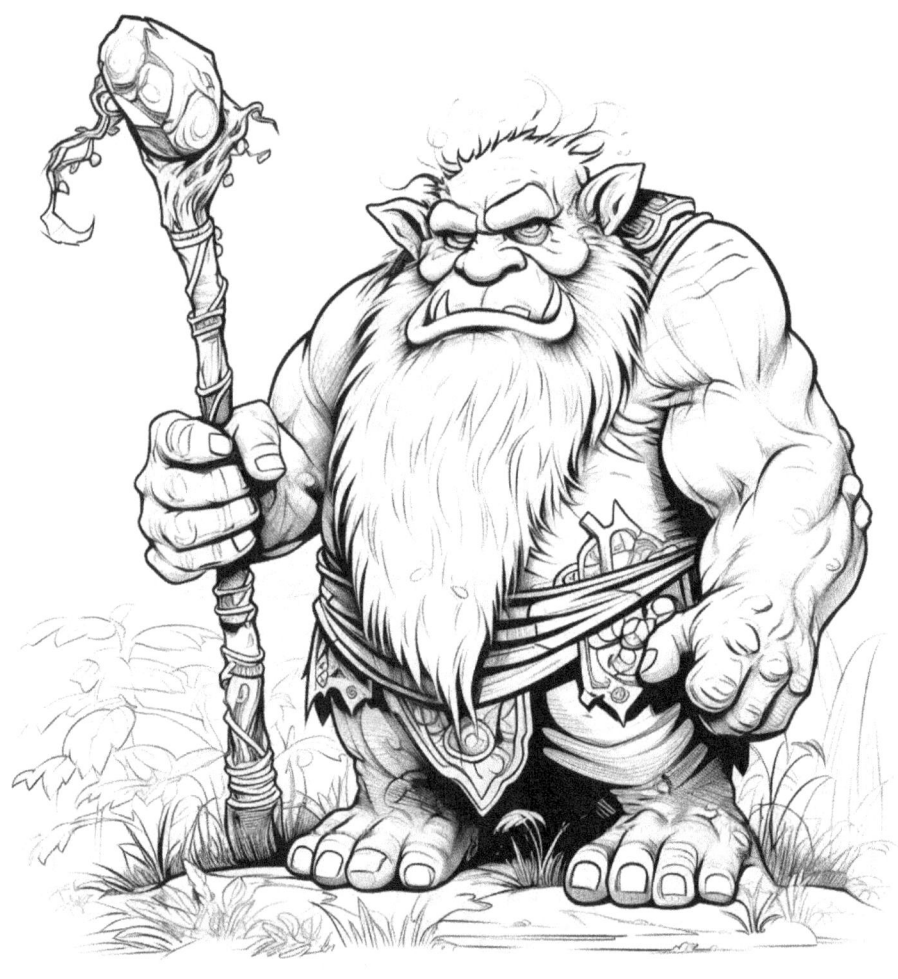

Write your story

World Fantasies Coloring Book

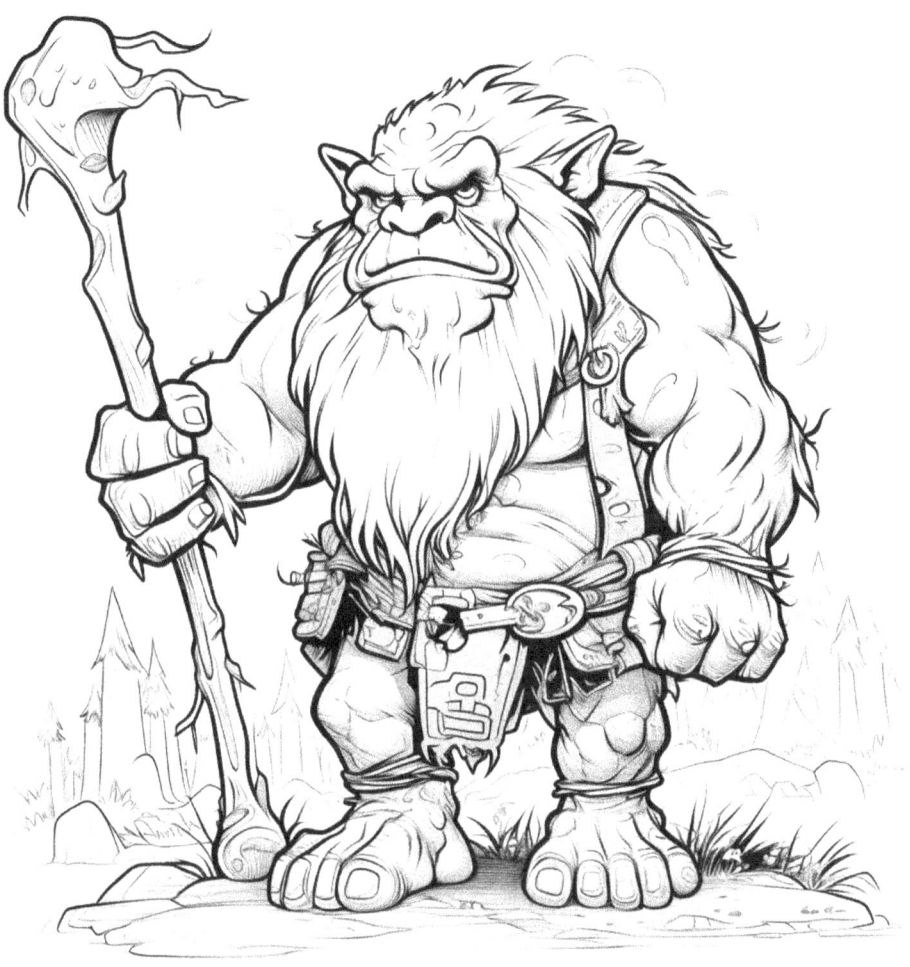

Write your story

World Fantasies Coloring Book

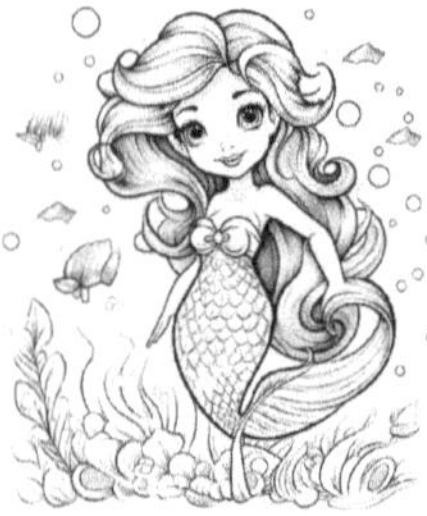

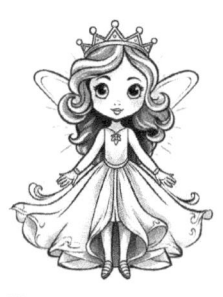
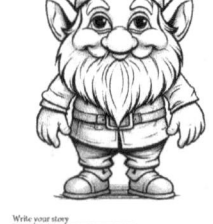

World Fantasies
Coloring Book

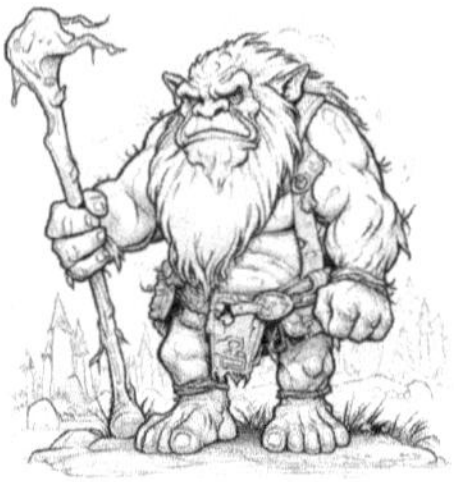

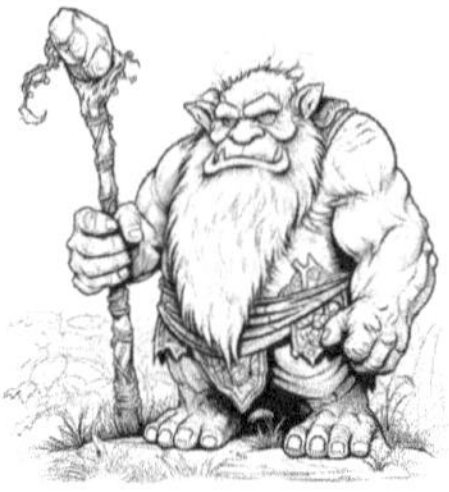

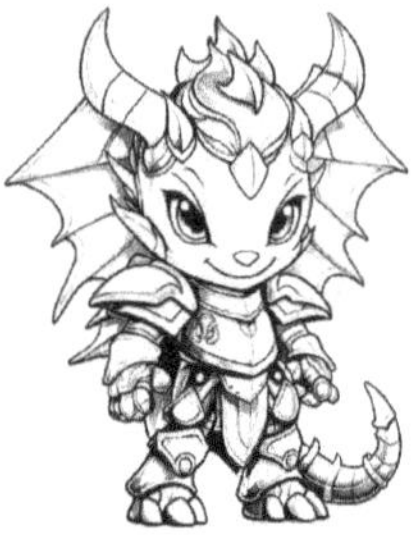

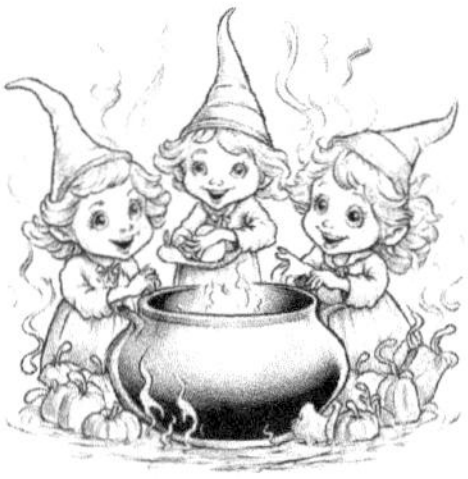

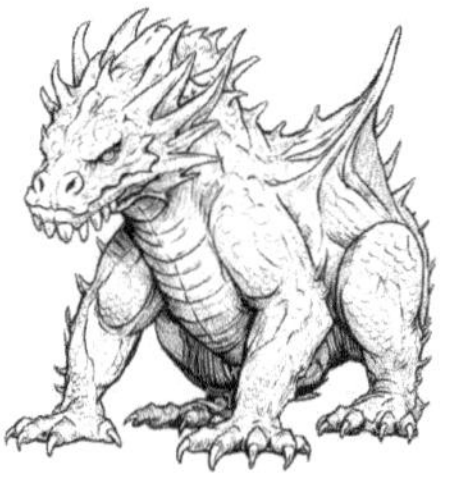

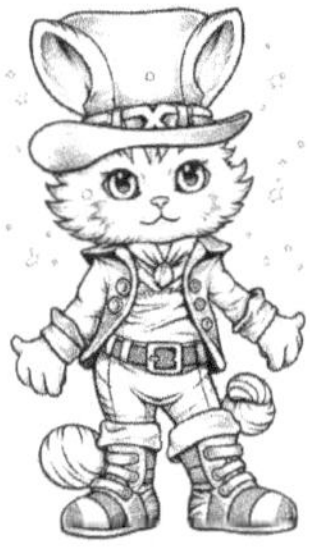

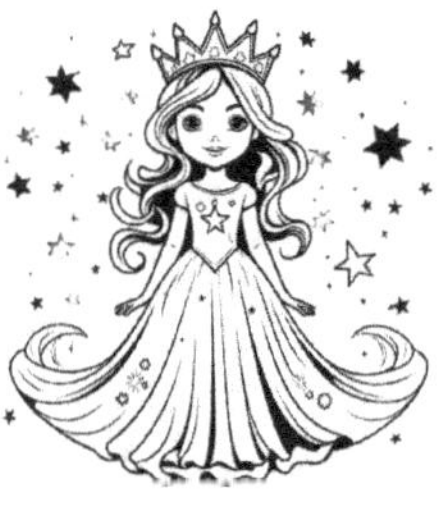

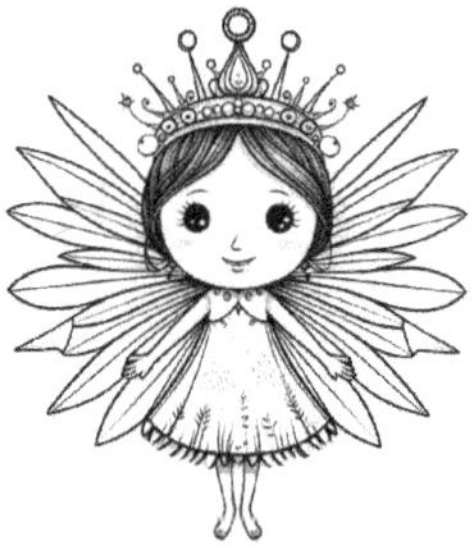

www.ingramcontent.com/pod-product-compliance
Lightning Source LLC
Chambersburg PA
CBHW030042230526
45472CB00002B/635